Praise for *The Story of Your*

"Like a new angel of history, *The Story of* arrives with its wings heavy with live fish and bone cake, faith and desire. Khalastchi has turned the poem into a long, beautiful wail, soft and brilliant enough for even Babel and Kafka and Singer to hear. It wouldn't surprise me to find out Khalastchi feeds each poem by hand, and brushes nightly their wings. With as much abandon as with hope, these poems sway on the edge of a miracle."—**Sabrina Orah Mark**

"It's *The Story of Your Obstinate Survival*, and mondegreen, malaprop, misremembering member these casted lines even as these lines cast a motley populace: holler at me wayward new Senator, honeymooners of the lusophone, mid friend, X-ray techs, and expecting pessimists. Expecting textual comic strips? Natch. Still catch the catastrophes beneath the cackling, between ill chimes and rhymes, the jinglejangle Daniel Khalastchi entangles in his syntax; he sets the lexical to play with itself roughly; sees the Locked-Downers stuffed in meat lockers; proffers ruefully to the newly born/newly gone: 'there is no use trying/to stop the wreckage.' Heck, all that glass and metal really sounds pretty."—**Douglas Kearney**

"*The Story of Your Obstinate Survival* lays out an uneasy dreamscape of middle-class, middle-aged life at what can feel like the end of a world. The immediate stuff and facts of that life—the roof, medication, cars, relationships, real estate agents, the occasional wild animal—all threaten to come apart in ways that feel as familiar as they do unreal or impossible. Through these strange scenes, Khalastchi rides sonic associations, hopes, regrets, histories, revealing an intelligent figure trying to puzzle out what it means to go on and finding little moments of humor along the way. This is a moving, compelling collection, a vital documentation of a life in uncertain times."
—**Heather Christle**

"When *The Story of Your Obstinate Survival* begins, the speaker—let's say there's just one speaker—of the poems has been dislocated from their body by an act perpetrated or instigated by a figure known only as the Senator, though it isn't immediately apparent that the Senator is responsible. The rest of the book reads like the speaker's attempt to sing their way back to oneness with their body, and though the attempt is colored by bewilderment, anger, and sorrow, it is as rich with music as any poetry being written today. *The Story of Your Obstinate Survival* is a triumph of song."—**Shane McCrae**

"Despite the personal and collective turmoil that stand back of Daniel Khalastchi's *The Story of Your Obstinate Survival*, the writing from poem to poem, line to line, is animated by linguistic joy and an almost madcap surrealism and humor that somehow manage to confront without prettifying or flinching from the nightmare of history, even while showing us how to maintain emotional and spiritual poise at the darkest of times."—**Alan Shapiro**

THE STORY OF YOUR OBSTINATE SURVIVAL

DANIEL KHALASTCHI

THE UNIVERSITY OF WISCONSIN PRESS

Publication of this book has been made possible, in part, through support from the Brittingham Trust.

The University of Wisconsin Press
728 State Street, Suite 443
Madison, Wisconsin 53706
uwpress.wisc.edu

Gray's Inn House, 127 Clerkenwell Road
London EC1R 5DB, United Kingdom
eurospanbookstore.com

Printed in the United States of America
This book may be available in a digital edition.

Library of Congress Cataloging-in-Publication Data

Names: Khalastchi, Daniel, 1980- author.
Title: The story of your obstinate survival / Daniel Khalastchi.
Other titles: Wisconsin poetry series.
Description: Madison: The University of Wisconsin Press,
    2024. | Series: Wisconsin poetry series
Identifiers: LCCN 2023040862 | ISBN 9780299348045
    (paperback)
Subjects: LCGFT: Poetry.
Classification: LCC PS3611.H33 S76 2024 | DDC 811/.6—
    dc23/eng/20231010
LC record available at https://lccn.loc.gov/2023040862

Dear reader, forgive me for not telling the story the right way.

—Isaac Bashevis Singer

CONTENTS

BRIEF EXPERIMENT WITH EXPOSITION

ELEVEN INCITING INCIDENTS

RISING ACTION AS COLLECTIVE MYTH

NINE ADDITIONAL COMPLICATIONS

TOWARD A HIGH POINT, OR ALL DOWNHILL

RESOLUTION

BRIEF EXPERIMENT WITH EXPOSITION

REPRESENTATIONAL INVENTION TO MASK
MORE SERIOUS EMOTIONAL CONCERNS

For the last three hours, I have sat on
your bathroom floor inventing a body

more able than my own. The model is
hardly functional, but it comes equipped

with the pull-string and edible crotchless
underwear you always said would serve well

to cover my poorly misidentified attachment
disorders. In its reclined position, the body says only

the few words I remember from my most recent
humiliating student evaluation forms. I had

hoped for more control, but the wiring
won't respond to water, or lighter fluid, or

my bold serrated nakedness trying to bring its
muscle some relief. From a radio I hear

an aversion therapist tell me *inside your lover's*
brother is the man her father will always wish you were

able to avoid. You are in the hallway or it is only
the police. This body, like others, I will leave

in emergency.

ELEVEN INCITING INCIDENTS

CONFOUNDING ATTEMPTS TO EXPLAIN THE MYSTERY

On a folded piece of
dead-red paper I

have written the
words *this tiger is not*

drunk enough to
kill us. I place

the piece of paper on
the lip of my used coffee

table, but you still
don't want to pet

the animal, and I still don't
want not to ask you

to. *There's something about*
the danger, you say, so

I pull out the
cigarettes and

gasoline and soon
the whole apartment is

burnt fur and sturdy
ROTC cadets all-hugging a

contaminated fire hose. I like
how your hair looks

in the loose mist of
that cold water, smoke

seizing with the shake of
what it means to hold

nothing. We don't know
if the tiger made it out or

where he will show up
next. When we get you

home, the Senator in
your bed suggests there

will always be the weight of
possibility possibly boxed

in what we never want
to open. You look back at

me, and I look down at
the blood now appearing

at the side of my right
ankle. *What is inside me?* I

ask. *What is inside me,* you
respond.

AMONG US A STOMACH

We step onto the highway and
suddenly you don't know what to do

with me. There are truckers in
skirts, cars parked in the drainage

ditch, and everyone is looking at
my beard and the wedding dress

I hold with my kneecaps as
you lean close and whisper *I just think*

they're hungry. I try to remind you that this
was your idea, but you are already walking

through the damp-set pavement like a
cat-calling female construction

worker in an all-girls tennis camp
bathhouse. I am cold and the light

is leaving and you look, even at
this distance, scribal in the sway

of your low-bare hips. As you
approach the crowd, I see we are

outside a convenient Mexican
restaurant. There are candles

in the windows, a man with no
legs, a child waitress asking

us kindly what we do not want
her not to bring. I put on the

dress in an attempt to age
respectably. One of the drivers

hands me a leash, and I bring
you a small goat that we tie

to a coat rack. When I sit
across from you, the crowd

we encountered stands ready
with cameras. I order you

a combination platter of two
speared fish and a warm

margarita, and after the plate and
glass are delivered you ask me to tell

you the story we haven't yet shared: *this
can't happen*, I say, paying in rhythm

the mariachi band to stop playing
"Borderline." You suggest I introduce

the other characters, but I argue
it's best if we skip to the end. *But*

this is the end, you say, and then you remove
a box from your purse and place it

weak on the table. There is an intercom
announcement requiring silence. What I

know of the box couldn't fit in an
airport. What I know of an airport just

takes you away.

AS YET

He says missus.   Miss
         us.   Miss egg
               tooth.   White.   Beak
      broke.   No

         break.   No mist
to mail   the letter seal.   He says
         missus I miss
      us standing.   Through

               walls.   Through
      litter.   Through light
         her cycle came
      not   not not.   He says

               missed her.   Miss her.   Miss
                  heard her hear
                        to calling.   Culling.   Pulling
                  him mister by wire,

               by tire, by why her she
         so misses   so tired.   He says
      liar.   Dealt.   Says
         delta is

rising keep
        nothing to hold.   He says
better.   Waits.   Listens
    again: more weight, more bets,

more bats, more lists.   He says
        our flood rose high
            black plumes
    in the night.   Says here

    we are startled. Both lost
    to the run.

YOU LEFT ADDRESSING HEADLIGHTS
SPENT IN ACTUAL TRAPEZE

Thrust in rust, the door of my hatchback won't hatch or crack open to allow any breath. All day, I sit in the car, or stand by the car, or climb to the roof of a new office building and talk with the smokers about what we can do for the gutted deer carcass now down in the polls. There's no real consensus but the sense left to get is that I am still senselessly bent toward a meaning. I parade in the parking lot lost in my costume, a riot of skin-smell of beard born to bear. Witnesses say perfumed in the radiant golf-carting heat I struck with a breaker bar blows to the windows a widowed wind owing these shattering knees. Such foraged need of water and what are we drinking? I never tried the other doors but heard back from the cardiologist that our aortic insufficiency is stable and unchanged. I tell my wife. I tell the paramedics. I tell the smokers on the roof of a new office building who breathe into brown paper bags from the co-op that everything here in our lemon grove growing is bitter and bitten and there is nothing to see.

DEAR _____: *I WANT TO BE A BETTER FRIEND, I'M SORRY*

You put your hand on my neck and
whisper that if you were here you would

sew me a telephone. *But you
are here*, I say, and then you walk

to the door. I follow your shadow past
my mother's gun-filled aquarium and

meet you on the porch where we watch a
slow wreck occur on the highway. The colliding

metal makes a severity of noises and we stand
admitting our own heroic transgressions

without ever discussing who let the neighbor's
kid unbury the body. When it's finally

dark enough to move in poor focus, you
saddle my shoulders with soldered toy

soldiers and ride me to the crash site so one of us
can flirt with the medical examiner about unsanitary

stock market projections. Nobody has enough
loose rope or batteries but the signs we've

made hold firm under the weight of your aging
chest. Lost in the panic we are ravenous

trumpets, mouths swelling like boxcars
to blow hard scissors and oil.

WE MUST BE SOLIDLY INDEMNIFIED

For better-bodied weather I fly
    with debt from coast

        to coast and roast my
            casserole of failures

        in an oven I still
        stomach. Cased Pyrex flexed

      against my thorax, I taste cold
the basted chicken, check

in on cheated heat, wait
      wading for my mission

        district colon to serve
            back. Landing near the water there

        are backhoes on the beachline
      in a ditched last pass to keep

      the roads from washing out. I stand in that
stock lighting and rinse away my

inbox, scrub the mass and pass
  on passing notes I wrote to say that

  I am married. Inside
    this cabin's habit I am

    habitually half
  bitten. To all the girls

  I loved before I never
bothered with your

birthdays. To the woman
  I now love I often wander

  by the shoreline wanting
    bread just like the rest of

    them, the clamor in my
  clavicle a sun we never see.

THE HYSTERICAL LIKENESS

I
Outside this basement
window is a second
window that looks
directly at a

II
box. The box contains

III
something not
worth much

IV
of anything. I want
you to open the box, but
you don't answer

V
my messages. There
have been times
these last seven-
teen days where

VI
I've wondered how
I got this weight-
lifting set or why

VII
I've been drinking
the Senator's Robitussin
mixed with all

VIII
this scotch. I have
in my hands two
tranquilizers. They

IX
do not help
me sleep. I take
them with me
to the gas station

X
and think about
the likelihood of
problematic communication
in the age of caged
physical

XI

contact. You do not read

XII

these. You do read
these but you do not wish to

XIII

respond. You do wish

XIV

to respond but
the effort to do
so spreads rust
in your chest. O-

XV

kay. You never asked

XVI

for this animal. But
what are we together if

XVII

not that?

REFRIGERATOR HUM

He says baby.   My
            table.   My
lady of
        harbors, of

        bathing by cables, I
        heard   you herding
    the tiger.   Here.   By my
                window.   Wind

        low.   Blowing my
        curtains, my
            captains, my
    crew   all lost

            to the roar of your
        beast.   He says
    meat.   Met.   Says
    we met and lost touch but

    kept feeling
        each other up
    late after parties.   He says
        partly.   Part

                me.   Says
                I never wanted this
        fire I'm
                sorry.   He says

shhh.   *Sleeping.*   Says here
                    in my dream you are
        littered with pets.   Pats.   She
                pats at her thigh he

                    stays in the bedroom.   She says
            fine.   I hear you.   Says
                    your sea is

        empty and
                no moon will find it.

BITTER AND BITTEN AND
THERE IS NOTHING TO SEE

To check against the testimony of chest-compressing generals, I broil in the kitchen a live chicken for the noise. Feathers hot in weather brought to purchase back our taxes, I sit in smoke and wake the now-choked neighbor with alarm. An arm it comes to me to see what I should not be doing, and while we concert-stream a border meme the chicken quick inside the oven orders Kaddish we can't give. Driver parked on silver tray the grave-dirt bird learns nothing more than mooring, the neighbor coughing lots in light of what we've lit for sight. I see aghast how grown the gas will pass us in the papers. Unsteady cross the room I move to lift aloft our fowl. Fixed ship against a swanning wall, the smell swells breached birth special counsel beaten ring. All of me is elegy, a house pronounced as sold.

IN TENNESSEE YOU TELL ME WE
ARE APPROXIMATELY SEASONAL

On top of that there was
            a murder: a car and a
                    bridge rigged up with
            hinged fencing; a man, and a
man, and a woman now

            suddenly gone. She was
                    the daughter of a father
            whose son went farther
with drugs than he
            ought have. She was the

                    sister of a brother whose
            mother gave out, gave in, gave
to her—your neighbor—the deed to the
            house. When she moved after
                    all that collapsing back

            home little was left but to swim
in those bedclothes—the never was
            made, the atomized cycle, the thunderous
                    sheets you could see from your
            kitchen. Based on what you've told me

about narrative, now is the time
to speed up the story: she mostly
was average—this woman, this neighbor,
in the overall
aggregate of how these things

go. She was herself after
gaining the house soon
married, soon divorced, soon
repartnered and parting each
day to her job

as an X-ray technician, peering
through bodies to her own found
crowned and distended in a river. According to the reports
you reportedly accessed, rocks bullied
her skin so bass-cracked and

heavy it was hard to know if
you wanted to keep hitting
the beats. Outside a Republican-
themed pizzeria on a highway
two-point-one miles from the

Historic Scott County Jail
where we agreed to spend our
evening, I watched you walk
toward our dinner dining
in shadows—your wife's

sprawling detachment, my wife's
        stalled appellate clerkship, our
friend pale-masked and buckled
in a rental car next to us, an
        Appalachian replacement of the

        Midwestern gestures under which
    we first met. I never heard the rest of
the shaman's web-net virtual death
        perspective or learned how the outcome
            turned out for your own children's

        benefit. Instead, we spoke with a
spirit who told us he wanted nothing
        but a cigarette, sang to a women's
            cell *grace can amaze*. When dawn
        purchased its furnace, we fled

to the car marking lists that could fit
        names of mythical businesses. For a moment
            at the wheel, we were the deer
        and the deer were the diners. We were
approaching the café where they

        were still eating. There was so much snow
            that no one was leaving. It is the absence
        of predators that believe in us killers.

GIRLS RUNNING IN THE SPRING

Some cars have rolled
their windows down

and I can hear
the music. Pushed

to me, it sounds
together both

at fall and al-
so rising; bass

from one low truck
in time with sing-

ing from another,
a tender love-

sick ballad made
technotic by

the hum. When these
cars leave their tra-

ffic I am some-
how less

attuned. From my bed
I hear a coxswain say

together pull
together. There is no

holding fullness
when the motion is

to spread. It's nice outside
and girls are running

away from me. There is a Honda,
Spanish music, pulling things apart.

RISING ACTION AS COLLECTIVE MYTH

YOUTH, AND OTHER MISGUIDED DIAGNOSES
OF A FAILED RELATIONSHIP

On the table are three sealed envelopes, a rubber
hammer, and a bucket of ineffective mood stabilizers

we've been keeping next to the Senator's discarded benefit
statements. We sit in hard wooden chairs for

more than an hour looking at the objects
and listening for a cop you say is still swimming

in the light fixture. The air in the room is stale
with rich humidity, and through a large picture

window we watch two bearded electricians put on
hospital gowns and tweeze each other's necks

one breath at a time. You make the first
move and reach for the hammer. I grab the

envelopes and soon we are standing on
the table yelling intelligently discursive

statements in a rhythm that shakes your face
in tiny defense: *The animals are learning!* you

say. *Everyone dies alone!* I respond. *This is our*
sad and fully realized future! you say, and then

a car appears unwed in the bathtub between
us. I think you want to keep yelling, or you think

I don't yell correctly, or we both get text messages
and I ingest all the medicine. In the morning, I sew

your jeans against your abdomen in a last-ditch
attempt for intimacy. There is so much

blood and then very little. You want a
squirrel in your mouth and I go out to find it.

ALL OF ME IS ELEGY,
A HOUSE PRONOUNCED AS SOLD

With aging contagion I take back my back to the
rental cap chiropractor practiced in fees. Alone
on me a sea-set collection ejects an elect sound
bound in my orbit, a store-bought port and barge
charging the ears. Here the room steers through
a clearing of cartilage, title-cut vertebrates bathed
without water. No body is free fed far from a
reason to learn as we turn toward who has a
spine. I mine my eyes and do not mind the doctor
and his absence. A sense is sent accordingly,
according to the invoice. Inside the room I stay
my weight and make to be examined. No one is
coming. My back is back to black and blue is back
to facing senators. A doorbell rings. A car alarms. I
sleep the sleep of honeymooners keeping peace in
Portugal.

DEAD TREE IN STAIRWELL

He says
    little.   Not
much.   Says
      it's   much as

      expected though
            I should sit
down.   Frowns.   He says
      I am in

garbage.   Cartons.   Says
    I see burnt   gardens of   carpets torn
up to the floor.   He says
      floored.   Knocked

over.   Says
    she found the floorboards and
      dug up her
    share.   He says

      shares.   Our
        business.   Says
          she when she shares it our
      business I'm

finished.   He says
    finish it.   Rest of it.   Rests
his face
   in a pile of

   coupons   clips
      to his beard
 some maps
and a list.   He says

   go.   Flee.   Says
  you can keep running and
      I'll buy a car.   He says
  care.   Cared.   Says   I don't

care what you say you're
      carrying my
  baby.   He says baby.   *Baby.*   Says
   I've fished

 for whole days
    without any water.   Says
  missus you know
    I come back   loaded.

ON VIEWING A SYMPATHETIC NAZI
PERSEVERANCE TABLEAU

When I wake up, you are standing
on the porch with the body of our

now-not-golden retriever cleaved from
belly to neck like an unsteady cancer

patient after seven long seconds
at a highly electric

rodeo. You refuse to take the dog
to the clinic, and I watch you pull

from its severed body a body of irrelevant
mass: wet muscle, tethered veins, a stack

of old quarters we kept buried in the yard
in case the addicts returned with the birth

of new weather. You throw the blue-red
mess near a pile of drowned kindling

and bring me the hide saying *please
put it on*. I try not to breathe or think

about the time the dog entered our
bedroom dressed as the Senator late

in the hours of a violent fundraiser. The fur
is coarse and I wear its disguise as you take out

a pistol and say *it's time for tricks.* Shots
come hot to the dead ground around

me and I pull to my knees and dance
with my waist and paws. You keep

shooting and I keep dancing and
then the county deputy arrives and you

lose your temper. When you get out
on bail, I drive us to the

river so you can sing Barry White songs
with a veteran for change. Around your neck

you keep a picture of my father's last
wallet. I promise, this collapse is coming.

FARING POORLY IN WATER

Run sick the mailman's trick
    is delivering the news: fire

        sale, sympathy card, multi-
      ethnic holiday bills we still owe

  the bank. Caught in breath-
      arresting winter I take

         the mail and fisherman's
        cake out to seed the flagpole,

    burying sweet salmon and
      paper next to the garlic

        bulbs we bought to feel sub-
      urban. Ground bound frozen

  rich with thick collected
    leaves, I pour gallons of

        steamed water and dig boiling
      my hands. I don't get far but

  far enough and stuff the treat
    and cancers down like laundry

in a soup bowl. Once everything
is covered it begins again

to rain. Dry, then damp, then
wet beneath my apron I ask

the photographing neighbor
who is winning this defeat. You

are maybe in the shower looking
down at me and singing. Why

do we have a flagpole? Where
does my sister get her parenting

skills? If we are both left in standing
water how is all of this ablaze?

TURNDOWN SERVICE

Somewhere in Virginia you are running
    with a colleague. Shoulders back rain

    still falling the two of you crowd through
wild blue indigo corporate in the same

new stayed trade commissions I imagine
    missing from our conversations over

    coffee. On the couch with your brother
I don't know why the cat isn't eating

in your absence or who the shooting
    news breaking one mile from where your

    grandparents are buried will bother. Cardinal
flower assault rifle hours this sinus

crushed heaving behavior is rich. Between us
    in actions we calculate credit by listing what

    charities bankrupt the time: you take
a bath and I measure my fingernails; I

sweater the cat with severed stale
    popcorn and you drink to a pony named

    Cupcake and sleep. As if this is how
we continue living. As if it always wasn't.

DEAR _____: *I WANT TO BE A BETTER FRIEND, I'M SORRY*

During the birth of your first child, I sat
folded in an unmarked commuter van selling

watered-down Novocain to the high school
boys cheerleading team just like you had

asked me to. Though your wife was initially
concerned by my persistent inability to properly

act in public when faced with the news of other people's
happiness, it wasn't as hard as one might think to adjust

my online dating profile to attract an attractive
dentist; to meet her for cocktails; to spend six

months saying *I am okay with waiting*; three months
fielding questions from her sister about my knowledge

of respectable, inelegant engagement jewelry. Once
we were committed to the face of something

civic, the keys and office access badges practically
arrived in gift baskets. The drugs themselves never

worked on me, but one night when I couldn't
find your phone number I drank small welts of the

leftover anesthetic and tried to pull out my
tongue with multifilament dental floss stapled to

a roaming city bus. *I can't lose
my voice for you* is a sentimental way to say

someone from your family will need to pay
my bail. How am I the one still living in this

town? The faucet is broken. Even the police
dog has a ring to remove.

GUTTER AND BRAIN

Inside the microwave are
          matches and lip balms
                    and sheets of aluminum

          foil cut to the shape of
your hands after sewing
          that flag of surrender we

                    never did raise. Because there
          is still room caught in the boxing, I add
waxed paper baggies and both

          halves of the spread-red Styrofoam
                    holder the medical handlers
          delivered with the organ

our surgeon had bet we
          couldn't quite get. Alone in
                    this winter beach-creaking

          commission, I need some kind
of fire to choke out
          the discussions I have

with my inbox. All of
the windows are closed and
sealed with convenience store

condiments. It smells of rot-picked
wood. I sit on the floor thick with
harvested kittens, the microwave

whirring a spark and its catch.

I SLEEP THE SLEEP OF HONEYMOONERS
KEEPING PEACE IN PORTUGAL

Turned away the mayors say our groceries are
brides: tied white, on special, picked up to be
let down. It's hard—although we argue—not to
name our disagreement. Away from home this
care alone is one regret of many. Making trouble in
the suburbs suffers fooling better moods. Moon,
you arrogant arranger of night-forgiving light, I
cannot sleep without you or my wife survived in
prizes. Disguised in bed an egret at the window
shows its shadow to the heat. There isn't anything
to see at sea, a governmental marriage. I am on a
littered beach awake and glittering with debt. In
the morning I will hunger for a table we can
purchase toward remorse. Distraction is an action
shown in humorous display. Thirteen hundred
miles from our mortgage we are running.

ANYTHING COULD BE BACK THERE

We send you to the desert with
a wet black box and two red

credit cards we agree you will not
not use even in the face

of such hormonally bruising
interest rates. It is hard

to explain the box to the people
you meet on the airplane—to the

captain, the wrestling team, the
woman you study in the aggressive light

of a concentrated bathroom—but once
you diagram the industrial

disruption of our recently speared
democracy, everyone agrees with

your need for such dramatic
escape. Later, through a message

I find in another man's laundry
basket, you tell me that after the

landing failed—after the gun
salute and sturdy rolling

blackouts—you flexed like a teenager
swimming in hay. Positioned on

this couch, I am polished in the
ceremony of a one-leg-braced poor-

footed defense. Your new Senator
has a map and the necessary anti-

biotics. If you climb in the box
you could ship you home. Breath so

white built cities of teeth. Teeth you won't
ever let go of your dinner.

OUR PREGNANT RACIAL OBESITY

Everyone helps drag the river while
we hold unfirm bananas in the wet
slice of your cleavage. Throughout

     the morning the fruit browns and
     bruises and after a time we are told
     to brace our weakening limbs with black

police batons. It is a female veterinarian
that first notices the body, bagged rice
heavy and shelved on the

     water. That night, the news is
     attractive and leads with a caramelized
     photograph of smiling lottery

winners. You and I take the doctor
to a dominatrix-themed collegiate
dance competition, and all three of us

     wear glittering face paint and hold keys
     to a boat we've been promised will get us
     laid. You say *where is this funeral not having*

its way with us? The crowd holds signs. We
act and react.

WITHERING FRAME

You hold the hatched end of a
Stanley PowerLock tape measure

and I swallow the spool so
together we have something to say

at the deposition. The chipped metal
casing makes me gag but I keep

down the lentils and am
able, minutes later, to ask for

things like advanced rust protector
and a new *Highlights* magazine without

sounding at all distorted. Throughout
the experiment you want to take

pictures of how the weight sits above
my colon—stomach distended, one

rib clearly broken, the belt clip
spooning against my appendix like a

desolate tree farm every time you pull
the reel. When a medical oddities

museum calls the next morning, after we
are intimate in ways that require us

to be separated by doctors, I am upset
that you have already melted down the

evidence and sent it off in an envelope
to the Senator who recently aroused your

interest through a vaguely racist
infomercial. Either way, I agree

to be a specimen in a digestive miracles
performance put on by a local community

theatrical group. On Wednesday
evenings, I ingest live fish and door-

knobs and nothing ever happens. The
checks are so manicured when they go

into my account. Sometimes we walk
again to the dentist and demand our jaws

be switched back. Other times, you call with
needs and I take in my hands six high-voltage

radios and stand in the shower so this can
be stopped.

THIRTEEN HUNDRED MILES FROM
OUR MORTGAGE WE ARE RUNNING

Spelt the field congressional my dinner has been
made a way of weary eating I cannot in spots
arrest. The plates are brought to table stable
porcelain in scores and serving after serving turns
our juried verdict bored. A mouth I crouch it
open still the worm is not without. It is raining
on our condo raining even on our plans. The
garden guarding flight risks tsks again at my
discordance. I order back the food now stacked
before me flooring servers. A doctor calls to
educate adjudicating ranges, says if I do not start
eating I'm a viral spiral down. Missing less I stand
impressed and fit inside this dress shirt, a vanity
embalming me in beige exchange of color. Closer
to the ambulance the chances of expansion span a
latitude too late. *She loves the unsigned border* reads
a tattoo in the *New Yorker* cartoon. A body book-
reviewed as clinical, the constituents debate.

FOR YOU ON YOUR BIRTHDAY

For your birthday
I've baked you
a cake of whole rabbit

and parsley. I didn't use
any yeast or flour but the cake
still rose because I left

all the bones in. There was little
preparation so don't feel bad
if it turns out you don't like

it. When I put the pan in the oven,
her fur caught fire. The flames set off
my smoke detector, but once I spread

her body over with mayonnaise
the hair singed dull and
everything got quiet. I caught

her in the courtyard
which means if you do end up
liking it I can try to catch

another one and we can cook it
together for our
anniversary. I used chocolate icing

but I'm sure you can see that
for yourself. I wanted to be with you
when you tried it, but I don't have

money for travel. None
of the innards were removed
so be careful when you cut

in. I remember one night
you said my bones moved in my skin
like a tent being raised

under water. I boiled her first so you'd
feel better about diseases. When it was
over, I clipped her toenails and

blew dry her coat, which I realize,
now, didn't matter. In
the kitchen, it smells

like wet wood and spilled
kerosene so I've opened a window. Your cake
should cool before I send it. If I can

get it to stay, I'll tie a blue
bow around its middle. If I can't
just know I really wanted to.

NINE ADDITIONAL COMPLICATIONS

VARIATIONS ON A LARGE HISTORICAL OVERSIGHT

There isn't a ladder, but there is a picture
of your new Senator in an airplane bathroom

holding a jeweler's saw against his
exposed stomach trying to cut out the

cancer. I don't know how you got the
hydrogen peroxide bottle past the hands

of so many calm Germanic janitors, or why
you held the camera with the knocked

rake of your shaved knees, but from what
the photograph shows there was turbulent

fever and the stewardess had given
everyone Plan B pills and shots of

Robitussin in case the procedure called
for a water landing. The perched laminate

flooring you both appear to be standing on is
covered in travel-sized tissue packaging and looks,

from some angles, like a rotisserie city built
wide into bone—a city in the mouth of a three-

legged cat, a cat fully held in an engine not
stalled. Your new Senator seems to be

saying something about the limited role of female
political correspondents during nationally televised

catastrophe fundraisers but you are holding
your own saw, carving at your own chest, removing

from yourself something you never really wanted in
the first place. We talk about this picture years later: you in

a bus checking children for lice, me in a botany
exhibit on blight. You say *where there isn't this loss I*

am lost in performance. I can't eat celery, I say. We watch
a boy swim in a flooded station wagon. When he comes

up for air, we are all in a meat locker.

A BODY BOOK-REVIEWED AS CLINICAL,
THE CONSTITUENTS DEBATE

Static statisticians purchase mortuary tickets in
advance of what the press has called *derivative
supply*. In ties these market analysts insist their
sisters blister, make cisterns of their bodies chests
collecting for a feed. What cannibal can't ride
this bull-black cross street back to bear? Barely
in my suitcase we are leaning not for birth. This
legacy of lost belief relieves a spare uncareful
bedding. Bright is not a sound I hear but fear its
gowned maternity. We don't want the child any
more than they might try to make us. Makeup on
a displaced tissue gives the family its chance. The
sea it rises steadily and suddenly arrives.

LAVA BY STAIRCASE

Okay she says. O-
 kay. You'd come
  to a crossroads and
   I shot your

 foot. I thought
  she says
  you were running
 away. Were getting so

    far ahead I
    had to do something
  drastic. She says
   Tragic. Habit. Says

I fell by misstep, you
 looked back
  with a sigh. She says
   site. *See.* Says

 when I saw you by
 sideways my
  muzzle was heavy. Brush fell
   around the scope-hole and you

never saw

it coming.   *Calming.*   She says
I came to claim
your things from the doctor.   Says I shook

him down for your wallet
and left.

THE IMMINENT DECLINE OF EVERYTHING WE'VE UNDERSTOOD TO BE WHAT GOVERNS OUR PRIVILEGED DAILY LIVES

I don't think you will leave me
      for the neighbor because

      I actually think you will leave
me for him. I think you will leave

me for the neighbor because I would
      leave me for him. I am hard to live

      with and this pandemic has a medic
made us in sudden need of. I sit around

the house, its bones a nest for
      me to wrestle in, and complain

      about my skin and back and order
unrequired items from the Internet to conscribe

my vanity toward the benefit of
      crisis. So when the neighbor stops

      by for a socially distant
cocktail—his recent separation

porched in his flowering eyes, his
      daughter's birthday parade recorded

      and available to view from
the safety of our living room like the television

binges we return to at night instead of
      finally reading the news—when

      he arrives and sits on our poorly tamed retaining
wall I see the dirt in his fingernails and his unset

hair and watch you smile at his ability
      to weather it: his wife gone in a fit, his

      job cut like a bad student
film. And yet even in this

dispassionate arena of unoriginal
      programming, he is here in our yard

      offering us his extra toilet paper. This kind-
ness is best described by your look

later as the two of you text about
      joining a CSA. In a teleconference

paid for by our employer's generous
medical coverage, my therapist

says that it would do me well to
    sell off my discomfort and confront

    these crashes in advance. The Wi-Fi
cuts out, but for a moment it looks

like she is putting on lip gloss so that
    we have something to get dressed

    for. You below me in the kitchen aren't
thinking of the neighbor or

if you are you are good at not making it
    the whale in our shared

    living space. But I am thinking of
the neighbor. His red mailbox. His

blue Jetta. His youthful catastrophic
    year and the infinite time he has

    ahead of him to make like it
never happened. We feel terrible

that the matzah we gave him
    wasn't approved to be used

    at the sacramental meal. It said so
on the box. But he wasn't

bothered. Don't you see why
    we should leave me?

DEAR _____: *I WANT TO BE A BETTER FRIEND, I'M SORRY*

We do not take our meals in bed because
we do not share one. From separate ships

we fight against an end to what the day will
never bring us—regulated social roles, a future

in banking, your face in a cage with my voice
as a bird. To better feel the night's un-

certainty, I sleep with a shovel stacked next
to my neck and dig for your umbrellaed legs

until I strike more solid matter. If there is a way
of bringing you this unraised home I've made I

am not sure we should know of it. Instead, alone
in this costume I lie cradled by laundry kept

lined like sad timber and pretend it is another
body. My father, say the doctors, no longer

has a colon. When I think of your new Senator I
see the white plastic spoon I swallowed at lunch

glowing in my abdomen seized heavy with
apology. The heat in this room keeps me always

awake. Someone writes a letter calling us a segregated
opera. I live in a cemetery. There is your light and

then there is nothing.

WHAT CHEER

I

During the accident, my foot
doesn't reach for the
brake. My hands release
the steering wheel and I

II

hold the white dog I bought
for you in my lap by the
neck. There is no use trying
to stop the wreckage. Glass

III

will break, metal will
moan, my unbalanced body
will hole the weak night and
there I will be in a tree

IV

with no organs. If I had better
prepared myself for the events
of this collision, I would have
taken more vitamins and swallowed

V

less restrictive familial obligation
in favor of modern growth. It
has been one year since I felt not
wrecked by the wreck of not

VI

an accident but by my displaced
personal decisions. I sit now
in this empty tree, two hundred
and sixty-five miles away from

VII

my grave decoration factory,
and cannot in any strong way
tell you I do not wish I was not
there. It is true that _____

VIII

is a name I have not said in
nearly _____ years, and it is also
true that every time I ever said
it I was speaking in some way

IX

to you. _____, you are
such a better bird. _____,
I am tired. _____, I have
learned to set myself within

X

your absence, and _____, as you
can expect from an unmanned
man like me, I do not enjoy
the pulse. Even without my liver

XI

and colon I sit in this tree—
the accident wailing still
below, the white dog now
strung from a schoolyard flag-

XII

pole—and I look at our old
house at our old jobs at my
mistaken missed
ache and wonder

XIII

in what world a dry lake and two
casino boats could get me somehow
back to that nearsightedness. Soon
enough a plane will take us down

XIV

to warmer weather and soon again
another plane will pull you across
the sea. I am not drinking,
_____. I am not taking the wrong

XV

pills. I am sitting in a tree,
my body unhinged, my car a
breached court out in view of the
neighbors. It will never work with you

XVI

to say that I am sorry. It will never work
with you to say that every mess
they cart away—every organ
now lost in the gutters of some

XVII

slate-roofed house, this nose
or pelvic bone, all of it, everything
together—has and still only reads
the function of you. The police

XVIII

officers come with ladders and the
firemen with guns. I thought I wanted
this terrible theater. Thought it would
save you from what I feared of

XIX

myself, but look at me now. At the space
between my arm and where my shoulder
should be. Look at me shudder
and ask everyone to stay away because I

XX

surely deserve it. If you listen to
the genealogists they'll say I have
no claim to history. If you listen
to me, I'll say this

XXI

is not a metaphor. That my wreck
wrecked you, your home, our us,
the victory board I still want to see
you win. I heard your new Senator once

XXII

say *the audacity of hope is in understanding*
that it is not forgiveness we expect
but an admission of the fact that—
factually speaking—forgiveness sometimes should

XXIII

not be granted. To that end,
I will admit that I am not asking
for forgiveness. That instead I am
looking at a body bag, a dog on a

XXIV

flagpole, at blood on snow on
lawns on metal fences and I
am really trying. What
else can the waiter do but bring

XXV

out the meat? How else can the
service attendant at the gas station
say *I'm sorry, we no longer carry*
those geriatric maps? I cannot ask you

XXVI

to come back to me because back
to me is not the relevant topic
being discussed. I have money
in a bank account and I have saved

XXVII

enough to buy a new body, a new
heart, new heat to sail the new
blood of my new cellular system more
quickly to my new and more refined

XXVIII

brain. I will do anything to cut
your grass when the summer
comes. To look you in the eye
and hand you a raven and ask

XXIX

of the bird *please Rabbi explain,*
and let you be the one to discard
the directions I've put in a tin
can that lead us back to a waiting

XXX

room of your aesthetic precision, to
a chair with many nails, at a time when
you think it is best to say *I understand where*
you are coming from and I have

XXXI

not yet decided.

A CONTAGIOUS AGE

Wearing all my clothes and
    wrist guards I stand driven in

      our driveway asking my
        sweet wife to hit me. She

        isn't laughing in our
      Volvo knowing now with

      some experience how swift
medicated changes come

to foreground such resolve. There seems
    to be an understanding that

      the best way to convince me
        I should not be stopped

        from action is to pass the Swedish
      engine by my shadow

      drawing air, a careful exercise
in accuracy we have tried

twice with the cat. It never goes
    as planned but planted

       in the pavement here there's little
          interest for investing time left to

       the particulars. Across the
    alley to the east I steal a retail

       conversation between renters
and sit down. I ask again my wife

to hit me and the Volvo revs
    in idle. A house

       party partially begins and soon
          it too will try my

          patience. There is a newspaper
    article in my back pocket

    I can't read with all this
anticipation. It discusses

drone attacks on foreign
    leaders but I cut it out

to mount the headline. It sounds
    like a high school band

    name. It makes me eager
for belief. My wife in

    accidental jackknife comes
to join me with balloons.

IT'S BEEN EVENING ALL DAY LONG

Just as blank I sink the bank beneath my
      grief of never having money. Here in this

      chandeliered cotillion-dealing weather
a white round light slight hanging over-

head casts taffy-asking shadows on the
      table where I sit, leaving me to wonder if

      what you really meant by *I can't stand*
to see you was that everyone is always

laughing at the oncologist's office. It
      probably wasn't, but now that you are

      youthful graveside I apply regret. Death I fear
is coming for my friends and my anterior

superior iliac spine. In the kitchen
      my wife is mixing collagen hydrolysate

      in a small cracked glass, the bald metal
spoon collapsing through the supplement

and ice, raising our flat-sat cat from a
      deep uncharted sleep. *Love is a boat*

combing over us with shame, and this
is what you told me when I asked

about divorce. *I'm not going to do it,* you
said, *but how else to handle weather?* The radio

hum is inaudible. There is no actual air to breathe
and yet our neighbor is still hosting dinner

parties. I am not a thief, but I have taken
time tonight to make a necessary

action. To whom are they going to send it?

THE SEA IT RISES STEADILY
AND SUDDENLY ARRIVES

Born radiant and ocular we press against
phoropters in hopes of helicoptering a hazy gain
in sight. Slight change a better gauge sees slit
lamps camped at the periphery, touching loose
a luscious contact to contract what we can't
read. For me I see the wall chart and think first of
mis-election, of opulent discovery still covering
the gaps. Income came before me stored with
porous morning breath and still the bills out-
shaped our sheep asleep in spoiled rent. If we look
at all the candidates through tired wire speculums
the speculation placed before us is our nation
needs a cane. Not able any longer loans accruing
through the phone, we recite the printed Lucite
and call delivery for clowns. Bright-colored noses
hair aware and stained lethargic we are lid plates
placed to hold a rolling out of scalpels. We ought
not want to see this but can't really look away.

TOWARD A HIGH POINT, OR ALL DOWNHILL

YEAR-END RECONCILIATION ADJUSTMENT

With the lights on, I walk back toward the
storage closet and remove a set of off-white

stoneware dishes and a pair of your proportionately
unflattering underwear from a box labeled "no

more dice." Next to the front door of my apartment
is a crude stick and yard-sack body I recently made by

repurposing lost hair pulled from the bathtub when
you were still sleeping here. The body doesn't

stand properly so I tape it to a curtain and
make inappropriate hand gestures

around the bottle of whiskey I've fastened
just below its belt. At a calculated distance,

the body looks enough like me to let
the scene play out—there is its thick-drawn

beard; its dead robin for a heart; its
mirror glued to its right hand reflecting

the real me, wearing your brassiere, chafed and red
along the shoulders. It is more difficult than

I imagined to be wearing your clothes and this
faux rabbit-fur wig, but since the election of

your new Senator, what else am I to do? Holding
the dishes in my hand, I throw the first salad

plate and scream *acute intellectual celibacy!* I throw the oval
serving tray, six misguided cereal bowls, a cup

with a state's inglorious motto crudely stenciled in gold
lettering between images of citizens and their often flooded

levy, but nothing ever breaks. One of the windows
behind the body starts to shake and someone calls

my cell phone to talk about a party. I take off
the wig and smell the still-whole terror of my living

space. There are fish under the washing machine in my
basement and that will make me famous. I am sorry

I never took anything from you or your belief
in me. The night isn't here. Won't ever now

come. For the record, if they ask, I will say this
was always the case.

DEAR _____: *I WANT TO BE A BETTER FRIEND, I'M SORRY*

Mama calls the doctor and the doctor says
this is a pattern we have warned you

about. I am on the roof again, belt tied
to a rope, rope tied to a truck, truck running

in the driveway, lights fixed on a deer. The
shadow cast by the animal is smaller than

expected, and my mother tells the doctor
that perhaps things are getting better. Since

I am not on the line, I can only imagine he
responds by bringing up the flood. She

is beautiful when crying, my mother, the matte-
gray night let loose around her overcoat, red-

rimmed glasses removed by her body's
collapse. This is when I see you waving from

behind the steering wheel. You are wearing racing
gloves, your bra pushed high in contemporary

fashion, a noose of your hair looped back on
my rope so that we are assured something wrong

will go right. The neighbors, once again, are
grilling small foxes. My sister and her children

are playing with a bat. If I could better see
your eyes, I would know if we weren't this time

only joking. Radio, we are electric. The current
is rising. I want you to drive.

OH, I THINK ABOUT THE DEAD

The rabbi fell in-
            to a gravesite and
    since then she's been

            communing. Every day
she calls the congregation's
            phone tree and talks of

        whose departed she's
            gone far with. Mr. Rabinowitz
        is first and we are told

            our long-gone gabbai
    is filling trenches on
a beach. Sunburned and

        cancerous he
            asked for this breached
    treatment because

his sisters baked in gas
            chambers while he made off
    to the States. He doesn't sound

himself, the rabbi says, but
still crowns us with
a tiding: he is stronger

in his shoulders stronger
even in his hips. We pass
along the information and

think who she'll speak
with next. Mrs. Pearlman
asks if she can pay to shower

insults at her mother. My
grandfather asks if he can
set appointments in

advance. The rabbi
has an aluminum cane
with four short feet praised

gray in solid rubber. I imagine they feel
like dentist chairs. Someone
on the phone tree says we must

give her a raise. At night, I dig
a hole and hold out what
we never know.

WE OUGHT NOT WANT TO SEE THIS
BUT CAN'T REALLY LOOK AWAY

Chest slapped across with pellet guns a
hamstrung man teaches us to shoot iguanas in a
raging kettled sun. Engraving great surveillance
we survey the very outreach of what property
we claim to name as assets for the bank: the title
deeds, the abstracts, the reacting proper taxes
stacked against us and our rafts. In defense we've
taken axes to the trees around our homesteads,
steady placing weighted cages as instructed
by control. Unfolding old prescriptions we
find kidneys kidding time, such massive acting
filters stained for general decline. Invasion is a
strong word for the worth we're here to stall,
tiled reptiles on the lawn a mile long and soon
surrounding. We don't want to kill the animals
but are told this isn't greed, isn't their association
fee to feed on or retrieve. Firm in ammunition we
are aiming rains of buckshot. Trying to I can't hit
anything yet the bodies pile up.

BECAUSE THE NIGHT

In this apartment, I am wearing nothing
but long underwear tied at the

waist with a belt I only recently
removed from a ceiling

fan now throwing rings of bent shadow
full across my bed. My nipples are hard, but

not in the *let's make this night
a night not to remember* kind of

way. If I put on a shirt, I know
I will stay in it—the glow

from the city pulsing through these
low-draft windows into my efficiency

like the machine at the bedside of our now-
not-dying famous writer's new home in

the South. Once, I talked to myself
about the practice of brevity in grave

moments of introspection. Instead,
tonight, I am at a desk, fastened to

a bookshelf, fastened to a wall, fastened
to a neighbor who uses a vibrator (or

something like a vibrator) when she
wants to get her dog's attention. There

have been so many moments and also
so few. I seem to only make mistakes

when I miss take the mistake
for an opportunity worth standing half

naked in my only room, sitting on my
only chair, writing to my only friend this

hell of letters to say the beat does
not always go on. James Franco once

said that *to be a master of the human
mind, the human must first mind what they*

cannot, with grief, disable. Okay. You're
right. James Franco didn't say

that, but the thought of him doing so has made
me remember that I have nothing. *Orpheus*

hesitates beside the black river. Will we
never see our dead friends again? If I had

to do the whole thing over again, etc.

A FORMIDABLE PLAN TO ADDRESS
THE NATIONAL CONVENTION

Cloth bag and basket-caddied the women
    in the checkout line don't believe

        I've bought enough to eat. Even when
    I share the contents of my convent-

renting ulcer, they ask to cook me
    dinner and who am I to wave away? We

        rustle in their Buick buckled in before
the speed bumps, and trunk the streets

    and beaches of South Florida toward
        home. There are so many deer lying

        face-flat on the asphalt it is one long
rug race to the carport until I realize

        they are palm leaves. I ask the women
        what I thought I saw but they are

          dis-entuned, focused rather on the
    daylight and how they'll make me

gain. Inside the kitchen of the house
　　I've been delivered, the range is

　　　　electric because gas is how their
　　parents died. In camps they tell me

they would eat torn cotton, and because
　　of this they have me lift my shirt up

　　　　after every bite I take. There is brisket
　　and cold kugel, latkes and white

　　　　fish. There is dark candied fruit in
　　　　Tupperware and I'm told to keep

　　　　　　it down. Each time I swallow, the women
　　confirm with a yard stick that it is harder

and harder to see my ribs, dead branches
　　floating under a solar-flexing pool

　　　　tarp. When I've beaten back enough
　　space onto the plates, we retire

to a bedroom and count our daily
　　pills. Who are, these women

want to know, my electable
contemporaries? For the first time

all night I hear my voice erect
a complex. It is a suite of

condominiums. They are over-
priced and underwater and if

I make it with the cavalry we
will sink from all the weight.

DANCE PARTY FOR THE END OF THE WORLD

Here in this drag city, ain't nothin' going on
    but the rent. I don't want

        to be a freak, but I can't help
        myself—I am alive with love, tripping

on the moon, coming out of hiding
    all evergreen and searching for sunset

        people. Right on target, I got the
        feeling to use it up and wear it out, to get

away from the visitors burning with fire
    and maybe this time dim all the lights

        right in the night and run away too
        blind to see it. I know there's something

going on—a private joy, a new attitude
    of brighter days—that leaves me feeling

        lucky lately, the power shame-free wicked
        game I love to love. Mercy, I got my education in

cha cha heels, bolero, unexpected lovers and I.O.U.
    souvenirs, more and more, the hitman higher

S.O.S. fire in the sky. In my house, the dominatrix
sleeps tonight and you are in my system, walking

on music, showing out. Take your time. Enjoy
the silence. Remember what you like, Angel

Boy, one night in a lifetime, a walk in the park. My heart
goes bang thinking of you. I can't help it. That's

the meaning in the bush, together in electric dreams.

AN INEVITABLE RESCUE

She says color.   Collar.   Call
    her to say the
    burns have healed,
then leave her

      with a check.   She says
          check that.   Stay.   Says
          check back later or
        wait for the beep.   *Beep*.   She says

      I am not here and you
          cannot make me so
          please stop sounding
        yourself in a hole.   She says

quiet.   *Quiet*.   Says my gift
    you took it
    now give me it back.   She says
      back now.   Tethered.   Pinned

      to a tenor or tent under
funds.   She says wait.   Can't
you hear me?   Says you were so
    hungry I   fed you my hand.

TRYING TO I CAN'T HIT ANYTHING
YET THE BODIES PILE UP

Crowds around the circus serve as means of
an escape, a legislative party bus of palliative
care. There standing by the advent tent are
penitential dentures, striking in their likeness to
entire choking towns. Backed down and bound
the carnival carnivorous is glowing, a midway
ways away alit and stilted by the night. Not today
is right for leaving but relief it never comes. A
sunken metal shtetel we are buried in our
phones, buried in our Eastern exodus under dust
percussive loan. Flown over, what is bypassed
loading homely in the dark? Our suitcase faces
forward toward a liver we can taste and the big
top stops its guessing weight the waiting all but
over. Stove caught the engine hot this highway
braids and bridges. Going anywhere aware is how
the Senator never leaves us. You left addressing
headlights spent in actual trapeze.

OUTSIDE THE HOUSE YOU SUMMARIZE

Light comes right slanted
 low my kitchen windows

  and I see you boarding
   plywood to the frame of

   your old door. Holding
  cake mix and a tooth-

  brush I walk outside to
bake in witness and watch

instead you demonstrate how to
  gamely swallow nails. One by

  one you place them in
   your mouth then chase

   with water, breath exhaling
  in a gale that I can palm along

  and hold. Coming closer
I see the nails aren't

nails but galvanized flat-
  saddled screws which

extend for us the metaphor
    you brought me here

    to learn. There is blood around
your mouth and on your

teeth when you stop
speaking. I tell you I am

not surprised she left us
    with no door to close

    behind her but that given
        the ox-pulled music

        box we're living in things
    could always have been

    worse. You don't laugh
or say anything about

the Senator's fraught
    relationship with sweating. I

    pretend not to call the ambulance
        and you pretend to use the

cake mix as a face paint
made for clowns. In the red-

blue lights your nose is
bright your smile is

extended. This could be
a rodeo if I were any good

at riding. Wide beneath
the night-pried sky I hold us

down the neighbor's watching.

RELATIVELY DIRECT LETTER OF RESIGNATION

There is a wreck on the
highway: two kids, a

deer, maybe two kids
of a deer and a badly lit

semi. Cars stall along
the pavement without

the proper condolence
cards. Everyone wants

out, or in, or out of what
they are in, and because

of this I unpack your bull-
horn and explain to the

mouthpiece all of my
elective shortcomings. I

have been such a horrible
man, and by man I do

not mean astronaut. There
are parts of a body one

can only give back to a
body. Other parts that

walk us like shovels,
stepping through night

slow marching the sea.

A STAIN ON ALL OUR HOUSES

First it was the Realtor knocking
quick against our door asking when
we planned on leaving. *Why would*

      we be leaving? we asked, and then
      she pointed to the stain. Next
      it was the neighbor drilling through

      the tasteless sheetrock saying he
      was eager to expand now that we
      were finally vacating. *Why would we*

be vacating? we asked, and then he pointed
to the Realtor, who pointed to
the stain. Then it was the census

      taker standing by our open window
      calmly stating that given recent errors
      in statistical significance she required

      names and ages of those living in the
      dwelling since we were no longer
      tenants. *Why aren't we the*

tenants? we asked, and she pointed
to the neighbor, who pointed
to the Realtor, who pointed to

the stain. After that it was the weather-
man, the barre instructor, the pundit
held in heels; it was the gallery

curator, the food deliverer, the barista
spelling names; it was the metro
guard, the hardware hand, the

child hauling kitty litter for the
Senator; it was the Senator, the
Senator, the Senator, the Senator, the

Senator, the Senator, the Senator, the
Senator, the Senator, the Senator, the
Senator, the Senator, the Senator, the

Senator, the Senator, the Senator, the
Senator, the Senator, the Senator, the
Senator, the Senator, the Senator, the

Senator, the Senator, the Senator, the
Senator, the Senator, the Senator, the
Senator, the Senator, the Senator, the

Senator, the Senator, the Senator, the
Senator, the Senator, the Senator, the
Senator, the Senator, the Senator, the

Senator, the Senator, the Senator, the
Senator, the Senator, the Senator, the
Senator, the Senator, the Senator, the

Senator, the Senator, the Senator, and the
retired ophthalmologist making sure we
saw the stain. It was crowded in our

      apartment, in the hallway, in
      the stairs. Taking out the paperwork, the
      Realtor said that even with the stain

      nothing saved us from the closing
      costs. *Why are we what's closing?* we asked. Everyone
      stepped closer to see what we would do.

POSTCARD IN DRAWER

Not mine are the days here
without you. I wake. Sit

up. Shower and brush
my teeth clean in a mirror; eat

at the table then wait
for the mail. Sometimes

this takes hours. Sometimes
whole days. Sometimes

I wake and I sit and I
eat and I wait for so long, I

forget when to stand and
I miss you-

r phone call. Last night, I sat
in my sheets with a flash-

bulb and camera but
couldn't find anything you'd

want to see in a picture. I haven't
swallowed right for days. My milk and my

water fall rough through my beard
and my pants are now pocked

like a spot-dying lawn. In my
chest, my ribs don't hold

nothing. Back home, I imagine you
swimming. You breathe

and you pull
and we somehow get closer.

DAYENU

If you had brought me out of wreckage
and had not given me land,
it would have been sufficient.

If you had given me land
and had not given me what was on that land,
it would have been sufficient.

If you had given me what was on that land   ,
and had not given me the understanding of what to do with it,
it would have been sufficient.

If you had given me the understanding
and had not given me the means to proceed with what I understood,
it would have been sufficient.

If you had given me the means
and had not given me the patience,
it would have been sufficient.

If you had given me the patience
and had not allowed me rest,
it would have been sufficient.

If you had allowed me rest
and had not allowed that rest to ready me,
it would have been sufficient.

If you had allowed that rest to ready me
and had not left me with directions,
it would have been sufficient.

If you had left me with directions
and had not given me a want to follow them,
it would have been sufficient.

If you had given me want
and had not given me the second try,
it would have been sufficient.

If you had given me the second try
and had not given me the water to try it in,
it would have been sufficient.

If you had given me the water
and had not pointed me home,
it would have been sufficient.

If you had pointed me home
and had not let me get there,
it would have been sufficient.

If you had let me get there.

If you had not been waiting.

RESOLUTION

MORE BAD NEWS

A phone call from
the insurance man
says my stunt went

terribly wrong:
the match took the
gas, the gas

took the fire, the
fire took the tiger
and the tiger found

guns. Men came
with water. The
neighbors brought

blankets. People
covered our good-loss
gallery and

tags were made
for the things that died
in fashion. Along with the animal

I'm told the possibility
banners we were making
got pretty hot and

gave in to the heat.
They didn't make it out
(nothing did) but

for what it's worth
we're covered. So
the apartment's gone.

So the framing
fell over and so
we have a death

toll. At least
we have pictures:
the ones of me

building, the ones of you
building, the ones of us
knotting the ground noose,

and the one of it working.
Somewhere
far from that field now

I see smoke haul up
and bridge a deck
pulled gently to the stars.

With a jar, I try to catch you.

NOTES

The title of this collection comes from Herman Melville's *Moby Dick* (Chapter 69: "The Funeral").

"What Cheer" (previously "'Til Mine—Emergency") was recorded and set to original music by Henry Finch for inclusion in the audio series "Lit Passages."

"It's Been Evening All Day Long" takes its title and interpolates a line from the Silver Jews song "Trains Across the Sea"; it is dedicated to David Berman.

"Because the Night" interpolates lines from Donald Justice's poem "There Is a Gold Light in Certain Old Paintings," Dean Young's poem "Thrown as if Fierce & Wild," and John Berryman's poem "Dream Song 28: Snow Line"; it is dedicated to Dean Young and Erik Lemke.

"Dance Party for the End of the World" is a collage of song titles from a Spotify playlist entitled "Dance Classics"; it is dedicated to Doug Powell.

ACKNOWLEDGMENTS

Thank you to the hardworking staff and editors of the following publications where some of these poems first appeared:

American Poetry Review: "Dance Party for the End of the World"
Colorado Review: "Among Us a Stomach" (previously "Your Mexican Stomach")
Court Green: "Refrigerator Hum"
Denver Quarterly: "As Yet"
Granta: "It's Been Evening All Day Long"
Mississippi Review: "Anything Could Be Back There" and "Because the Night"
Octopus: "More Bad News"
Paper Brigade: "The Imminent Decline of Everything We've Understood to Be What Governs Our Privileged Daily Lives"
Poetry Northwest: "Representational Invention to Mask More Serious Emotional Concerns"
Shankpainter: "For You on Your Birthday"
Thermos: "Year-End Reconciliation Adjustment" and "The Hysterical Likeness"
Verse Wisconsin: "Confounding Attempts to Explain the Mystery" and "Variations on a Large Historical Oversight"

...

The journey to complete this book relied greatly on support, guidance, and love from my family and friends:

Without pulling me to shelter, this book would not have been written. Thank you to the Hermitage Artist Retreat, its staff, and my fellow residents.

Without the rations and the map, this book would not have been written. Thank you to James Galvin.

Without lighting the way, this book would not have been written. Thank you to David Kajganich, Sabrina Orah Mark, Doug Powell, and Vinnie Wilhelm.

Without responding to the flares, this book would not have been written. Thank you to Thomas Agran, Kyle Beachy, Dan Beachy-Quick, Jackie Biger, Heather Christle, Ed and Mary Conlow, Zach Isom, Douglas Kearney, Nam Le, Stephen Lovely, James Marcovis, Amy Margolis, Shane McCrae, Tracy Meginnis, Erika Meitner, Caryl Pagel, Josh Parkinson, Sevy Perez, Marc Rahe, Chicu Reddy, Justin Schoen, Alan Shapiro, Lindsay Vella, and my parents (Bobbi and Nashi Khalastchi: באהבה, בתודה, והערצה).

Without the welcome home, this book would not have been written. Thank you to Sean Bishop, Jesse Lee Kercheval, Jackie Krass, Dennis Lloyd, Allie Shay, Ron Wallace, and everyone at the University of Wisconsin Press.

And without the home to get to. Thank you to Kate Conlow—
"wherever people gather, her deeds speak her praise." I love you.

Wisconsin Poetry Series

Sean Bishop and Jesse Lee Kercheval, series editors

Ronald Wallace, founding series editor

How the End First Showed (B) • D. M. Aderibigbe

New Jersey (B) • Betsy Andrews

Salt (B) • Renée Ashley

(At) Wrist (B) • Tacey M. Atsitty

Horizon Note (B) • Robin Behn

About Crows (FP) • Craig Blais

Mrs. Dumpty (FP) • Chana Bloch

Shopping, or The End of Time (FP) • Emily Bludworth de Barrios

The Declarable Future (4L) • Jennifer Boyden

The Mouths of Grazing Things (B) • Jennifer Boyden

Help Is on the Way (4L) • John Brehm

No Day at the Beach • John Brehm

Sea of Faith (B) • John Brehm

Reunion (FP) • Fleda Brown

Brief Landing on the Earth's Surface (B) • Juanita Brunk

Ejo: Poems, Rwanda, 1991–1994 (FP) • Derick Burleson

Grace Engine • Joshua Burton

The Roof of the Whale Poems (T) • Juan Calzadilla, translated by Katherine M. Hedeen and Olivia Lott

Jagged with Love (B) • Susanna Childress

Almost Nothing to Be Scared Of (4L) • David Clewell

(B) = Winner of the Brittingham Prize in Poetry

(FP) = Winner of the Felix Pollak Prize in Poetry

(4L) = Winner of the Four Lakes Prize in Poetry